G000109732

Memoirs of Major Oldfield; Extr. from His Own Papers and Various Public and Private Documents
by Thomas Oldfield (Major.)

Address:
HardPress
8345 NW 66TH ST #2561
MIAMI FL 33166-2626
USA
Email: info@hardpress.net

P

P

MEMOIRS

OF

MAJOR OLDFIELD.

MEMOIRS

OF

MAJOR OLDFIELD.

MEMOIRS

OF

MAJOR OLDFIELD;

EXTRACTED

FROM HIS OWN PAPERS,

AND VARIOUS

PUBLIC AND PRIVATE DOCUMENTS.

" He was buried amongst us, and carried with him to the grave, the esteem of the French army."
                                        BERTHIER.

FOR FAMILY CIRCULATION ONLY.

DARTFORD:
G. A. POCOCK, LOWFIELD-STREET.

MEMOIRS,

&c.

THE subject of this memoir was born at Stone, in Staffordshire, on the twenty-first day of June, 1756; he was the third son of HUMPHREY OLDFIELD, Esquire, an officer in His Majesty's Marine Forces. His mother, whose maiden name was NI-CHOLLS, was descended from an ancient and respectable family in Shropshire, where they possessed considerable property; this property, at the death of Major-General Nicholls, (who took the name of Broadhurst,) was divided and sold. The Major-General was in the Honourable Company's service. Major Oldfield, according to family tradition, was descended, through * Sir Anthony Oldfield, from Oldfield of Oldfield, in the

* Created a Baronet August 6, 1660.

county of York, the heiress of the elder branch of which family married John Monckton, of Melton-super-Montem, in the county of York, Esquire, a Major in the service of Charles the First, and ancestor of John, first Viscount Galway.

Oldfield of Oldfield was descended from Aldred de Alfeld, or Aldfeldt of Aldfeld, in the county of York, whose son Radulphus was (as appears by the Monasticon Anglicanum) a benefactor to the Order of Knights Templars at a very early period. The family is of Saxon origin: the name has been variously spelt at different periods; indeed, in more than one instance, it has been differently spelt in the index and in the text. That Sir Anthony and the Major are from the same stock, the Patents for Armorial Bearings leave little doubt: the lineal descent, however, from Sir Anthony, requires proof; and the Major's pedigree, as recorded in the College of Arms, goes only to the Rev. Edward Oldfield, who married Miss Aston in 1665. George Martin Leake, Esquire, Chester Herald, who was employed by Capt. Oldfield, to make out his claims to the title, as a descendant from Sir Anthony, writes, (in March, 1827): "After every possible investigation has "been made, you appear to be the only "person who can have any well-grounded "pretensions to the Baronetcy." Some idea of the difficulty of proving a descent may be formed from a letter of the Rev. Mr. Fowler to Capt. Oldfield, transmitting some extracts from parochial registers, and wherein that gentleman writes: "In short, Sir, there was, at this period, "such a total want of order and regula- "rity in keeping the registers, and such a "shameful practice of cutting out leaves, "and inserting others in their place, as to "give too much ground for suspicion of "some unfair proceedings at the time, "and to the injury, as I fear it may prove, "to yourself and others."

Humphrey died in America, shortly after the affair of Bunker's Hill, in which he was engaged: he had three sons and one daughter: his eldest son, Edward, and his daughter, Jane, died young and unmarried. John Nicholls, his second son, served on the Staff, with the 63rd Regiment; with a Provincial Corps; and in the Marines, during the American War: upon his marriage with Miss Hammond, the daughter of an officer in the Navy, he retired from the service; and died in 1793, leaving one son, John, an officer in the Corps of Royal Engineers, born May 29th, 1789; who married, first, the daughter of Christopher Arden, Esq. of Dorchester, (formerly an Officer of the 19th Light Dragoons,) and Miss Churchill, daughter of the Rev. C. Churchill, of St. Thomas, Exeter; and, secondly, Alicia, daughter of the Rev. Travers Hume, D. D. and Elizabeth Hume, of Lissanoure Castle, in the county of Antrim, niece and heiress of George, Earl of Macartney.

Thomas, the third son, and the subject of this Memoir, accompanied his father to America, in the autumn of the year 1774, or in the following spring. He served as a Volunteer with the Marine Battalion, in the affair of Bunker's Hill, on the 17th June, 1775: in this action he was twice wounded; first, by a spent ball, which struck him in the breast; and, secondly, by a musquet ball, which passed through his wrist, (the use of which he never perfectly recovered); notwithstanding the severity of this second wound, Mr. Oldfield could not be prevailed upon to quit the field. The Marine Battalion, commanded by Major Pitcairn, conducted itself upon this occasion with the gallantry for which this most valuable corps has ever been distinguished: it suffered severely: its Commandant was killed; and * Major Short, the second in command, died a few days afterwards, from excessive fatigue.

Mr. Oldfield, immediately after the action, accepted a Commission in a Provincial Corps, it is believed, Tarleton's Legion. In 1776, he was, by mistake, appointed to the Marines, a Commission intended for his brother being made out in his name: the Provincial Corps giving only temporary rank, he was recommended to take up the Commission, and his brother received another as soon as the mistake was explained.

Thomas, who never joined the Marines until the close of the American War,

* A near connection of the Hammond family.

served with his brother (an Officer of Marines, but doing duty with the 63rd Regiment) at the siege of Charlestown, South Carolina, 1780. The brothers had never met, from the period of Thomas's embarkation for America, until the army was moving upon Charlestown to form the siege in 1780, when they rode together for a considerable distance on the line of march; mutually pleased with one another's society, on parting they exchanged addresses, and thus became acquainted with the near relationship subsisting between them.

Thomas was promoted to a first Lieutenantcy in the Marines, on the 16th of April, 1778; being very soon distinguished by his intelligence and gallantry, he was placed on the Staff of the Quarter-Master-General's department: some copies of returns as Deputy-Assistant-Quarter-Master-General, found amongst his papers, are inserted in the Notes.

As Deputy-Assistant-Quarter-Master General, he was attached to the Head Quarters of the Marquess, then Lord Cornwallis; and to Lord Rawdon, afterwards

Marquess of Hastings: constantly engaged under their immediate eye, he was by them deservedly and sincerely esteemed; they repeatedly bore testimony to the zeal, gallantry, and ability of Major Oldfield. The former, in recommending to Government, in 1799, the claims of his nephew and adopted son, after eulogising his conduct in high life, concludes by saying: " that gallant officer has now lost " that life I have so often seen him hazard " in the service of his country."

Mr. Oldfield was taken prisoner with Lord Cornwallis, at the capitulation of York Town. During the American War he was several times wounded; thrice taken prisoner; and thrice shipwrecked. The second time he was shipwrecked, was on the coast of America; he preserved his life by swimming, and was the only person saved from the wreck; he was taken up by a boat, and carried on board a ship, in which his brother happened to be embarked, and in which they were subsequently cast away together.

At the termination of the American War, he embarked on board a man of-war, and came to England as an Officer of Marines. On his passage, he was attacked by a pet bear, belonging to one of the officers of the ship, and was with great difficulty released from the animal's grasp.

Mr. Oldfield, about this time, sailed with Sir Henry Trollope, who took great pains, and succeeded in breaking him of an impediment in his speech. An old connection had subsisted between the Trollopes and the Oldfields, as appears by the Visitation of the County of Lincoln, A.D. 1634, registered in the Heralds' College.

Upon Mr. Oldfield's return to England, he was, with his brother, quartered at Portsmouth. Their intimacy with the Coffin family, contracted during the American War, induced them to purchase, as a shooting box, a small cottage, (Oldfield Lawn,) in the parish of West-Bourn, in the immediate neighbourhood of Stanstead, the residence of Mr. Barmell, who married Miss Coffin, and over whose extensive and well-stocked manors they had the privilege of sporting. For this cottage Major Oldfield always retained a strong partiality, and had projected considerable additions to it, had he returned from Syria.

About the year 1788, Mr. Oldfield embarked for the West Indies, from whence he returned in nearly a dying state. In 1793, he lost his brother, whose only son he from that time adopted as his own: in this year he was promoted to the rank of Captain; and a second time embarked for the West Indies, in the Sceptre, 64 guns, Captain Dacres. On Captain Oldfield's promotion, he disembarked from the Crescent, 32 guns, Sir James Saumarez.

Captain Oldfield, in 1794, commanded the Marines landed from the squadron to co-operate with the army in the Island of St. Domingo; he was then under the immediate orders of Colonel, afterwards Lieut.-General Whitelocke, as appears by a letter (in the notes,) directing him to withdraw from the post of Cote-de-Fer, where he commanded.

Captain Oldfield distinguished himself on every occasion that offered; in storming one of the enemy's works at Cape

Nicolas Mole, he was the first to enter it, and with his own hands struck the enemy's colours, which are now in possession of his nephew.

Captain Oldfield a second time very nearly fell a victim to the climate, and returned in the autumn of 1795 in a very precarious state of health.

In 1796, Captain Oldfield was employed on the recruiting service at Manchester and Warrington, when by his zeal and activity he procured upwards of one hundred recruits within a twelve month; upon leaving the recruiting service, he embarked on board the Theseus, 74 guns, and sailed to join the squadron, under the orders of the Earl of St. Vincent, off Cadiz; upon the Theseus reaching her destination, she became the flag-ship of Nelson, then a Rear-Admiral.

Captain Oldfield was engaged in two bombardments of Cadiz, in the month of July 1797, in one of which, being in the boat with the Admiral, he was slightly wounded.

Immediately after the second bombardment, the Theseus, accompanied by a small squadron, sailed for the Island of Teneriffe: in the gallant but unsuccessful attempt upon this island, Captain Oldfield commanded that portion of Marines which effected a landing from the squadron; the boat in which he was being swampt, he swam on shore, and in landing, received a severe contusion on the right knee, which did not, however, prevent him from exerting himself with his accustomed zeal and ability. By his conduct he materially contributed to the saving of the British detachment, whose temerity in making the attack with so inferior a force, was only equalled by the gallantry and intrepidity with which they carried it into execution; its failure may, in all probability, be attributed to the misfortune which happened to the Fox Cutter, 10 guns, which was sunk by the enemy's fire, with a considerable part of the force destined for the enterprize. In a narrative of the affair, written by Captain Miller of the Theseus, he states that Captain Oldfield not only distinguished himself as an Officer, but in more than one personal conflict with the enemy.

The British loss on this occasion was very severe, (141 killed and drowned, and 105 wounded.) Sir Horatio Nelson lost an arm; and Capain Bowen, a very distinguished Officer, was amongst the slain.

Captain Oldfield, in a private letter written after the battle of the Nile, speaking of that great action, says, that "it was by no "means so severe as the affair at Tene-"riffe, or the second night of the bom-"bardment of Cadiz."

Until the Theseus was detached to join Sir Horatio Nelson, (who, after the affair at Teneriffe, had shifted his flag to the Vanguard, and was sent by the Earl of St. Vincent in pursuit of the French squadron up the Mediterranean, Captain Oldfield remained with the fleet, under the orders of the Earl of St. Vincent, with whom, as well as with General O'Hara, the Governor of Gibraltar, he was on the most intimate terms: the former had been an old friend of the family, in Staffordshire, and was brought up with Captain Oldfield's maternal uncles: the latter he had served with, on the Staff in Carolina and Virgi-

in which County they had left no considerable property, as well as in Yorkshire and Lincolnshire—

nia, in the American War, ~~where they once possessed considerable property~~.

At the Battle of the Nile, Captain Oldfield was the senior Officer of Marines in the fleet, and on this occasion obtained the rank of Major, his commission as which was dated Oct. 7, 1798. The following account of that memorable action is extracted from Major Oldfield's letter to his sister; it is confined to the part taken by his own ship, the Theseus, and blended with matter of a personal nature: " On " the first of August, when, after sitting " down quite disappointed at not finding "the French fleet in Alexandria, the Zea- " lous made the signal for its being in the " Bay of Aboukir; the Steward was put- " ting on the table the last bottle of wine " for the day, when the Officer on watch " sent down to tell me the Zealous had " made the signal: joy was instantly seen " to illuminate every countenance. I or- " dered my servant to bring me a clean " shirt, and dressed immediately: at half- " past three, we saw them all very plain- " ly: at half-past four, the Admiral " hailed us, and desired we would go a-

" head of him: this order was instantly
" and cheerfully obeyed. The Admiral
" bowed to me, as we passed him; I never
" saw him looking so well:—at forty-five
" minutes past six, we were alongside the
" Guerrier, within seven yards of her.
" Our first broadside carried away her
" main and mizen masts; her deck was
" completely cleared; there was only one
" Frenchman to be seen, he was on the
" starboard gangway. We passed on to
" the Spartiate, and anchored abreast of
" her; ten minutes afterwards, the Admiral
" anchored on the other side; about half-
" past eight, we perceived the L'Orient to
" be on fire; at ten o'Clock, she blew up,
" and nearly 800 of her crew were de-
" stroyed by the explosion; which was
" awfully grand.

" The French lost by this action, including
" those who died of fever, nearly 5000 men,
" exclusive of prisoners. After the action
" I was sent with my Marines on board the
" Tonnant, and from the first to the four-
" teenth, I never undressed, but to change
" my linen, and only laid down occasionally
" on the deck. We had upwards of 600

" prisoners on board, of whom 150 were
" wounded. I certainly expected to have
" taken the fever, which made great havoc
" amongst the prisoners, but, thank God, I
" have escaped. I have heartfelt pleasure
" in saying my Officers and Marines behaved
" very well; and I am confident there was
" not a ship in the fleet better manned than
" we were. Providence was certainly very
" kind to us; our loss was but trifling. The
" poop was very much shattered. * Beatty
" and myself had one shot which knocked
" the plank from under us. Most of our
" poultry were killed, and the arm chests
" beat to peices. I was nearly overboard
" during the action; the rope attached to
" one of the davids by which we hoist up
" our boats caught fire, I went forward to
" extinguish it, some guns firing at the
" same moment from both the upper and
" lower decks, caused a concussion, the
" shock of which was so great that it nearly
" threw me overboard.

" An Officer who came off from the shore
" with a flag of truce told me their fleet
" was better officered and manned than any

* One of his Subalterns, now Major Beatty.

" that had sailed from France since the Re-
" volution. I do not think there is another
" Admiral in the service who would have
" attacked them except the Earl of St. Vin-
" cent. Sir Horatio Nelson sent to me two
" or three messages, to say that nothing
" would give him greater pleasure than to
" serve me: I sent him word I wanted no-
" thing."

Major Oldfield received some severe con-
tusions in extinguishing the fire alluded to
in his letter.

The British force at the battle of the Nile
consisted of ten ships of 74 guns, one of 50,
and a brig of 14 guns; the French force, of
one ship of 120 guns, three of 80, nine of
74, and four frigates; of these only one ship
of 80, one of 74, and two frigates escaped
the action; these were afterwards taken.
The British lost 218 in killed, and 677 in
wounded.

The Theseus remained for some time at
Gibraltar and Lisbon to repair the damages,
which were considerable; early in the following spring, she sailed to join Sir Sidney
Smith off the Coast of Syria.

The following relation of the siege of

* St. Jean d'Acre, from the period of its
investment to Major Oldfield's death, is
translated from the narrative of General
Berthier, Chef d'Etat, Major of the French
Army in Egypt. The siege was raised on
the 21st May, 1799, after sixty-one days'
open trenches; and thus, through the
energy, conduct, and gallantry of Sir
Sydney Smith, Bonaparte received his
first, and for many years, only check; he
was then, for the first time, opposed by
Britons, and completely foiled in his attack upon a Turkish town, fortified with
little more than a wall and round tower,
garrisoned by Turks, and a few hundred
Seamen and Marines.

" On the 18th March, the army and
head quarters marched upon Acre: the
roads being bad, and the weather hazy,
it was very late before the army arrived
at the small river of Acre, which runs
in a deep and marshy bottom: as the
passage appeared difficult, and the enemy's Tirailleurs, both horse and foot,

---

* An historical note upon St. Jean d'Acre, in the
appendix.

showed themselves on the opposite bank
of the river, Bonaparte did not think
proper to effect the passage until morn-
ing : during the night, a bridge was con-
structed, and the army passed the river on
the nineteenth."

· "The General-in-Chief immediately caused
a height to be carried, which commanded
the town, at the distance of a thousand
toises, and the enemy to be driven into the
town, from the gardens surrounding the
place, and in which they had taken post."

" The army encamped upon an isolated
height, which ran parallel to the sea, at
the distance of two thousand yards, extending to Cape Blanc, a league and a
half to the northward of St. Jean d'Acre ;
and commanding, to the west, a plain,
bounded by the mountains which run between Acre and the river Jordan."

" On the twentieth, the Generals Dom-
martin and Caffarelli, made a reconnoissance of the place, and decided upon
attacking the salient angle of the east
front: during the reconnoissance, the Chef
d'Brigade, Samson, of the Engineers, was
wounded. No intelligence had yet been

received of the embarkation of our siege artillery.

" On the twenty-first, we broke ground, 150 toises distant from the place, advantage being taken of the gardens, of the ditches of the old town, and of an aqueduct connected with the glacis of the place."

" Posts were established to confine the enemy within the town, and to repel his sorties. The breaching and enfilading batteries were commenced, and the approaches continued with great activity. On the 27th, the enemy made a sortie, and was repulsed with loss."

" On the 29th, the breaching and enfilading batteries were completed: the battering train not having arrived, the field artillery, consisting of four twelve-pounders, eight eight-pounders, and four howitzers, were placed in battery."

" At break of day, they commenced battering in breach the tower on the front of attack : about three P. M. a breach was effected. A mine had been sunk, to blow in the counterscarp ; it was sprung, and the desired effect believed to be obtained."

" The impatience of the troops decided
Bonaparte to order the assault : the breach
was supposed to be similar to that at Jaffa :
the grenadiers advanced with eagerness,
but were arrested in their progress at the
edge of the ditch, which was found to be
fifteen feet deep, with a good counterscarp; this obstacle did not abate their
ardour; ladders were placed, and the
front files descended into the ditch, but
on arriving at the foot of the rampart,
they found the breach still eight feet
above the rubbish. The Assistant-Adju-
tant-General Maillé, scrambled up to the
breach; he was killed at its summit. The
fire from the place was terrible; the counterscarp had prevented the advance of the
detachment destined to support the advance, who were consequently compelled
to retire."

" The enemy were, at first, panic struck,
and fled towards the harbour, but they
were rallied, and brought back to the
breach, where the bravest troops of
Djezzar were collected."

" The height of the breach above the
rubbish, prevented our grenadiers from

immediately mounting it, and gave time
for the enemy to return, and get on the
top of the tower, from which they hurled
large stones, grenades, and combustibles
of every description upon our people.
The grenadiers, after getting to the foot
of the breach, finding themselves unable
to mount it, retired, with the loss of six
killed, and twenty wounded. The Adju-
tant-Generals Lescales, and Languiere,
were both killed."

"The taking of Jaffa had created so much
confidence in our people, that the defences
of Acre were considered of much less importance than they deserved; the ditch had
not been well reconnoitered; the counterscarp was considered only as a slight obstacle; it was believed to be in ruins, and
in many places nothing more than a slope
from the covert-way to the foot of the
rampart; such was the ardour of the assault that, without examining the effects of
the mine, it was considered to have completely succeeded, whereas it had only
made an excavation in the glacis, in place
of blowing in the counterscarp."

"On the 31st March the enemy made a

sortie, but was repulsed with considerable loss. The Chef d'Brigade of Engineers De Troyes was killed. Djezzar sent his emissaries to Aleppo, to Damas, and to the Naplouzians, with a quantity of money to levy en masse all the Musselmen capable of bearing arms; he announced, that we were but a handful of men, without artillery; that he was supported by a formidable English force; and that they had only to come forward in order to exterminate us. We were informed by a party of Christians that a large body of troops were assembling at Damas; and considerable magazines of provisions collected at the Fort Tabourie, which was occupied by the Maugrebins. Djezzar was in momentary expectation of the arrival of the troops from Damas, and consequently encouraged to make sorties."

"Having continued to batter the breach, and succeeded in blowing in part of the counterscarp, Bonaparte ordered an attempt to be made to effect a lodgement in the breach of the tower, but the enemy had so filled it with timber, sand bags, and bales of cotton which our shells had set on fire, that it was found, to be impossible."

"We awaited the arrival of our siege artillery, and a supply of ammunition, to enable us to form another attack; during this time, we were occupied in pushing a gallery under the tower that was breached, in order to blow it up. The work being of great importance, the enemy, who had discovered our men, used every endeavour to destroy it, but without effect."

"On the third of April, our siege artillery had not yet joined us, and we learnt that three vessels of the convoy, laden with provisions and ammunition, had lost themselves in a fog, and got amongst the English squadron, by whom they were captured. Several pieces of siege artillery having been taken in these vessels, Bonaparte sent orders to Admiral ~~Pener~~ *Perit.* and to Damietta, to replace them."

"The English Commodore, seeing that the troops of the Pacha had been repulsed in several sorties, projected, in concert with the French Colonel of Engineers, Philippeaux, a general sortie upon

our works, in which the British were
to bear a-part."

"At day break, on the seventh of April,
the enemy sortied in three columns, upon
our right, upon our left, and upon our
centre; at the head of each column, was
a detachment of British Seamen and Marines. The batteries were entirely served
by the English, and their colours were
displayed with those of Djezzar. The
enemy purposed to surprize our advance
posts, but he was perceived, and received
with a smart fire from our parallels; all
who appeared were either killed or
wounded, and the right and left columns
retired without gaining an inch on our
works."

"The centre column fought more ob-
stinately; its design was to penetrate
to the entrance of our mine; the command of it had been intrusted to Major
Oldfield, a distinguished officer, who with
some of his intrepid countrymen advanced
boldly to the entrance of our mine; they
attacked like heroes, and were received by
heroes; death alone checked their bold

career; the rest fled, and took shelter in the fortress."

"The reverse of our parallels was covered with the dead bodies of the English and Turks."

"The body of Major Oldfield was carried off by our grenadiers; they brought him to our head quarters; he was at the point of death, but on his arrival he was no more; his sword, to which he had done so much honor, was also honored after his death; it remains in the hands of one of our grenadiers; he was buried amongst us, and he has carried with him the esteem of the French army."

The official dispatch of Sir Sydney Smith; the various public accounts of the siege, both English and *French; have not failed to eulogize the gallant conduct of Major Oldfield.

The Major's death was first communicated to his sister-in-law, by a letter from the British Minister at Constantinople, which will be found in the Appendix.

* Amongst the French accounts, see Dictionnaire Historique des Sièges et des Batailles Mémorables, tom. i. p. 26.

Captain Millar, R. N. commanding the Theseus, in announcing his death to Mrs. Oldfield, thus expresses himself:—

"It is with infinite concern, I undertake the mournful task of relating an event, which I am too well assured will occasion you the deepest sorrow; the death of your very worthy and gallant brother, and my much esteemed friend, Major Oldfield, who fell in the enemy's trenches, in a sortie, made the seventh instant, from the town of St. Jean d'Acre. It is some consolation that he experienced no bodily suffering: the wound which deprived me of an inestimable friend, and his country of one of its best and bravest officers, was instantly mortal."

Captain Millar was killed shortly afterwards, by the accidental explosion of some shells on board his own ship, the Theseus.

Upon the fall of Major Oldfield, the Turks, who had retired, rushed forward to recover the body: after a short, but severe conflict, they were repulsed, and the French carried off the body; which was buried by them with military honors, at the foot of Mount Carmel.

In person, Major Oldfield was of middling stature, dark complexion, eyes, and hair; he was of a social disposition; possessed of great generosity ; ever ready to proffer his assistance to those that needed it; an excellent man; an affectionate brother; the best of uncles; a kind and firm friend; a good master; a perfect gentleman, and a thorough soldier. It might be said of him, as of the Chevalier Bayard, that he was "sans peur, et sans reproche."

It was a maxim which he inculcated on his nephew, and which he himself practised, "that there was nothing in this world worth doing a mean action for; much less, an unjust one."

He possessed a strong sense of religion, and fulfilled his moral duties with great exactness.

A tablet, in memory of Major Oldfield, has been erected in the Garrison Chapel, at Portsmouth. The Lieut. - Governor, Lieut.-General *Sir Hildebrand Oakes, in

* Sir Hildebrand's letter is in the Appendix.

granting permission for its erection, availed himself of the opportunity to express the high sense he entertained of his merits.

Major Oldfield's faithful servant, William Crawfurd, whom he had remembered in his will, died a pensioner in Greenwich Hospital, into which the Major's family had procured his admission.

Napoleon, when on his passage to St. Helena, spoke of Major Oldfield's gallantry, to the Marine Officer on board the Northumberland.

APPENDIX.

This and the following documents are merely inserted to corroborate the text.

Return of the Waggons, Horses, and Boats, of the Quarter-Master-General's Department at Gloucester.

September 9, 1781.

	Boats.	Batteaux.	Waggons.		Forge Waggons.	Ox Team.	Number of Horses.
			Large.	Small.			
Complete and fit for Service.	1	2	30	6	1	1	144
Total.	1	2	30	6	1	1	144

3 Conductors
44 Waggoners
12 Artificers
10 Negroes for Boats

(signed) THOS. OLDFIELD,
A. D. Q. M. General.

Original sent to Head Quarters.

" York Town, October 10.

Dear Oldfield,

Be so good as to wait on Colonel Dundas, and give him every assistance in your power to acco-modate two hundred sick, ordered to Gloucester, this evening at dusk.

All the large boats are ordered to go to Glou-cester, they shall be sent as fast as possible.

Commodore Pratt and Serjeant Taylor, shall be sent under your directions, to assist in taking care of the boats.

Yours, &c.

(*signed*)   R. ENGLAND,

Major, A. Q. M. Gen.

Lieut. Oldfield, A. D. Q. M. Gen."

&c. &c.

" Mole, 15th April, 1794.

Sir,

Since your departure last night, the repre-sentations that have been made to me respecting the post under your command, induce me to order you to evacuate it with your whole force, this day, at half-past three o'clock.

Captain Walker, I send for the express pur-pose of destroying the guns in the most effectual manner possible. The houses and all the build-ings whatsoever may be destroyed in as great a degree as the time will permit; but nothing should retard your march beyond half-past three o'clock.

(*signed*)   I. WHITELOCKE,

Lieut. Col. Comm.

Captain Oldfield,
    Commanding the Station, Coté de Fer."

"Constantinople, 10th May, 1799.

Madam,

Under such a pressure of public business, so multiplied and laborious, as not to admit of my writing to a single friend or relation, I feel it a sort of sacred duty, not to let a public Gazette be the first vehicle of such melancholy intelligence, as the transmission of the enclosed letters must sufficiently prepare you to expect from the lines, which I have, I may say, created the time to scribble, in order to spare you such a poignant shock, as you must experience at the sight of Major Oldfield's name, in an Admiralty List of the unfortunate champions of his country's cause, on the Coast of Syria. Commodore Sir Sydney Smith's dispatches, passing home through my hands, I have been in the way of becoming thus pre-informed of the circumstance, and loss attending an attack made by the French, about the 8th past, upon Acre, defended by the force Sir Sydney Smith had thrown into that place, from his own ship, Le Tigre, and from the Theseus and Alliance.

The enemy, near ten thousand strong, commanded by Bonaparte in person, were repulsed in a way they have been little accustomed to in their previous campaigns; but this success has been dearly purchased, as Sir Sydney Smith feelingly describes it, " by the loss in slain and wounded, " of the flower of the three ships, amongst whom " the brave Major Oldfield is honorably classed." By the same packet, I received a letter from the squadron, which made me acquainted with your address, and determined me to send back the two others enclosed, which were on their way to the Theseus through my hands, when they were thus lamentably arrested by supreme decree ; but I must stop, or I shall defeat my purpose, and, in giving way to my own feelings, harrow yours; for I have no less than three relations, including Sir Sydney Smith, on the identical spot, for whose fate I am kept in constant suspence: and even with the knowledge of several severe affairs having happened since the melancholy event which forms the subject of this letter, I am in utter darkness as to the details, or whose name will swell the new black list, I am in hourly expectation of receiving.

In case you should be prompted to reply to this letter, or may wish to make use of my channel, for any enquiries analogous to the subject in question, I most willingly offer you the free use of my cover, and the best offices my situation here can enable me to render you on this mournful occasion, to which effect I beg leave to inform you, that my address is to the care of Messrs. Farquhar and Co., Bankers, St. James's Street, London.

I have the honor, &c.

(*signed*) SPENCER SMITH.

Mrs. Oldfield, Portsmouth."

" Portsmouth, 28th May, 1805.

Madam,

I was favoured with your letter of the 25th instant, in consequence of which I went myself to examine the Garrison Chapel, and have given directions to Town–Major Grant, that the monument you wish to put up to the memory of your late brother, Major Oldfield, shall be placed in the church, against the wall on the left of the pulpit.

I beg leave at the same time, to express the gratification it affords my feelings, that I have it in my power to assist in doing honour to the memory of an officer, who gallantly fell in a siege so memorable as that of St. John d'Acre ; and who behaved with such distinguished courage, as to draw down praises even from his enemies.

I have, &c.

(*signed*) H. OAKES.

Mrs. Oldfield, Woolwich."

NOTE UPON THE CITY OF ACRE.

The City of Acre, anciently termed Accho, Acre, and by the French, St. Jean d'Acre, from its being the residence of the Knights of St. John of Jerusalem, is the most southern city on the Phœnician Coast; it was a considerable city in the time of the Israelitsh Judges, since we find the Tribe of Asher could not drive out its inhabitants, (*Judges*, chap. i. verse 31.)

It having, in process of time, been enlarged and beautified by Ptolomy the First, was called from that circumstance, Ptolemais; the Greeks, however, amongst whom the last name was generally used, did not forget its ancient name, but softened it into Acre, calling the place indifferently by both names, until falling into the hands of the Turks, it resumed its ancient name of Acre, by which it is now called.

After being in possession of the Emperor Claudius, it fell into the hands of the Arabian Turks, who kept it until the Holy War; when it was retaken by the Christians, A. D. 1104. The Turks took it again under Saladin, and it was wrested from them in 1191, by Guy, King of Jerusalem; Richard I. King of England; and Philip of France; it was then given to the

Knights of St. John, who held it for nearly a century, with great bravery; but the Christians disagreeing about the possession of it, Sultan Melich, with an army of 50,000 men, obliged its inhabitants, in the year 1291, to give up the place, and retire to the Island of Cyprus.

Acre was immediately entered, and plundered by the Turks, who made a horrid slaughter of those that remained in the city, razed its fortifications, and destroyed all its noble edifices, as if they could never take sufficient revenge on it, for all the blood it had cost them.

Acre, by its excellent situation, seems to enjoy all the advantages to be derived from sea and land; being encompassed on the north, and east, by a fertile plain; on the west, by the Mediterranean; and on the south, by a large bay, extending from the city to Mount Carmel.

THE END.

PRINTED BY G. A. POCOCK, LOWFIELD-STREET.

Check Out More Titles From HardPress Classics Series In this collection we are offering thousands of classic and hard to find books. This series spans a vast array of subjects – so you are bound to find something of interest to enjoy reading and learning about.

Subjects:
Architecture
Art
Biography & Autobiography
Body, Mind &Spirit
Children & Young Adult
Dramas
Education
Fiction
History
Language Arts & Disciplines
Law
Literary Collections
Music
Poetry
Psychology
Science
…and many more.

Visit us at www.hardpress.net

WS - #0218 - 050824 - C0 - 229/152/6 - PB - 9781318534913 - Gloss Lamination